WHAT IS WRONG WITH SOCIAL JUSTICE

ELGIN L HUSHBECK JR.

Energion Publications
Gonzalez, Florida
2014

ISBN10: 1-63199-083-7
ISBN13: 978-1-63199-083-0

Energion Publications
P. O. Box 841
Gonzalez, FL 32560

energion.com
pubs@energion.com

INTRODUCTION

Social Justices both infuses and shapes our society. Individuals, community organizers, and union leaders advocate it. Spiritual leaders such as pastors, priests, and even the pope teach it. Thus, it should be no surprise to find city, state, and national politicians, along with governments and world organizations such as the UN, also playing a strong role in this seemingly ubiquitous movement. Who could be against it?

I am, and this short work will briefly lay out some of the problems with Social Justice. It will start by looking at the concept itself, what do people mean by 'Social Justice.' Since many of its supporters see religious obligations for Social Justice, the second part will look at its biblical basis. We will then examine how destructive the theories of Social Justice are when put into practice. In doing this, we will see that Social Justice is questionable in theory, wrong scripturally, and harmful in practice.

When presented with such evidence, supporters of Social Justice knowingly or unknowingly often resort to the irrational fallacy of an ad hominem attack; that is, they label detractors as uncaring, or in some cases greedy, selfish, or even racist. To counter this error, the last part will sketch an alternative approach that I believe is more rational, biblical, and, in fact, already has produced far better results.

Given the constraints of the Topical Line Drives series, i.e., short, focused discussions on a question or topic, one should not expect a full and complete analysis. Many books have been written on the definition of Social Justice alone. A quick search for books on Social Justice at Amazon.com returned over 100,000 results. Here I can only outline the basic arguments.

Also, while Social Justice is not limited to economics, that will be the main focus of this discussion. So there will be nuances and qualifications that, given the limitation of space, I will not be able

1

to address. Likewise, there will be objections to my claims that I am well aware of, but again did not have the space to address, which will be particularly true in Part IV. Thus I will close with a further reading section for those who want to explore these arguments in more detail. What I do hope is that this short book raises some questions about Social Justice and points the way towards a better approach.

PART I: WHAT IS SOCIAL JUSTICE

When we start looking at Social Justice, the first thing we need to do is understand just what we are talking about. Along those lines a key point is that Social Justice is not Justice. While it is theoretically possible that Social Justice could be a type of the broader concept of Justice, that is not the case.

If the word "Social" in Social Justice merely functioned to describe a category or type of Justice, then it would, in most respects, be completely unnecessary. After all, why not just call for Justice? Why limit the call for Justice only to the "social" area? There would be no need for the term "Social" as Justice is Justice whatever the area.

The reason supporters speak of Social Justice instead of simply Justice is that the 'Social' in Social Justice is a modifier. Social Justice is not Justice in a normal sense; it is a modified Justice. Since it modifies Justice, it is no longer real Justice at all. If you need to add a modifier to the word Justice, you no longer are talking about Justice, but something else. Whatever Social Justice is, it is not Justice.

One only need look at the writings of its supporters to see this. As a report from the UN puts it, "Present-day believers in an absolute truth identified with virtue and justice are neither willing nor desirable companions for the defenders of social justice" (Department of Economic and Social Affairs, 2006, pp. 2-3).

When dealing with the more theoretical aspects of Social Justice, things are not quite so stark. "Two of the most prominent statements about Social Justice" (Robinson, 2014) are John Rawls in his book *Justice as Fairness*, and David Miller's *Principles of Social Justice*. There is considerable merit to a lot of the arguments these authors put forth. But I think they do go wrong, as does Social Justice, in a few key areas. One of these is pretty clear in Rawls' title: *Justice as Fairness*. The other is the third of Miller's three elements of Social Justice: Equality (the first two being Need and Desert – in the philosophical sense of something deserved).

To some, this may seem very puzzling. In 21st century Western culture fairness and equality are seen as extremely positive values. After all, who wants to be unfair or support inequality? An additional problem is that all these ideas have become so intertwined as to make discussion difficult. Thus, some now define Justice as that which is fair and equitable. To understand why these terms are so problematic we first need to come to a better understanding of a few key ideas.

Say Justice and most people think of courts, and the two are, or at least should be, closely linked. By understanding how courts have evolved, we can come to a better understanding of Justice because there is a consensus that modern courts, while not by any means perfect, are considerably more just than in earlier centuries.

Three key factors differentiate modern courts from earlier ones. The first is a greater reliance on objective evidence. Eyewitness testimony can be affected by a whole range of factors. Fingerprints, DNA, and similar types of physical evidence are given greater weight because they are more objective. Objective evidence is important, as a critical component of Justice is the truth. The second is clear rules that govern the process, again in the attempt to make it more objective, and to reduce abuses.

The third factor is the concept of the Rule of Law. The Rule of Law is a large subject area and given its abstract nature can be difficult.[1] Here, let me just summarize it by saying that the Rule of Law is defined by two key concepts. The first is that laws are fixed, clear, and known. In short, they should be objective. The second is summarized in the phrase; no one is above the law. Regardless

---

1 See *Preserving Democracy*, chapter 4 for a more complete discussion.

of who they are, everyone is to be treated the same, which is why traditional statues of Justice are of a woman carrying a balance scale in one hand to symbolize the weighting of evidence and a sword as a symbol of power in the other, and since the 17th century blindfolded (Kennedy, 2010) to depict objectivity.

At first glance, this may seem to be in agreement with the defining principles of Social Justice, fairness and equality, but there are some significant differences. When one considers the concept of "equal" in terms of people, it must be within a given context because people are individuals and thus are inherently unequal. Not everyone, for example, is equal in age or height. So when someone says people are equal they must include how they are equal. We must ask, equal in what sense?

While equality before the law is an important characteristic of Justice, equality before the law is a particular type of equality. The advancement in the Rule of Law is that no special consideration is given for one's position in life, sex, economic status, education, etc., and giving any is seen as an injustice, which was not always the case.

While the focus of equality in Social Justice is not limited to economic factors, economic equality or inequality is a major concern of Social Justice and puts Social Justice in conflict with Justice. While a utilitarian approach would seek a social system that sought the greatest good for the greatest number, Rawls argues for an approach that would seek the greatest good for the poor.

Such an approach is not unreasonable, and, in fact, has great appeal. But it is not Justice. While Justice is blindfolded, Social Justice tries to tilt the scale in favor of the poor. As former Senator Herb Kohl once summarized it, "The neutral approach, that of the judge just applying the law, is very often inadequate to ensure social progress" (Prager, 2012, p. 215). While Social Justice's concern for the poor is worthy of praise, its weakening of Justice is cause for concern.

Where things get problematic is when the issue of fairness enters the discussion. While, as we just saw, equality has some issues, most Social Justice theorists are not seeking to eliminate all

4

economic inequality. While not all would agree, Miller's theory, for example, includes what he calls needs and deserts. Needs are those things required to live while deserts are things one can get by working hard. While everyone should get the needs, Social Justice does not demand that everyone get the deserts. Miller's theory thus allows merit based inequality as long as it is fair.

The problem enters in when trying to determine what is fair and unfair when it comes to economic inequality. There is agreement among supporters of Social Justice that the current system is unfair and thus that the current levels are unjust. But it is very difficult, if not impossible, to get any consensus on what would be fair.

This is a problem with fairness. It is an extremely subjective term, particularly when it comes to economic issues and thus it should not be a surprise to find that determinations of what is fair varies widely from person to person. A large part of the variability comes from the information considered when determining what is fair.

For example, when determining whether a price is fair, should the focus be on the work and effort that went into making the product or should the focus be on the ability of the person wanting it to pay the price? These could lead to vastly different answers to the question of fairness, but it hardly ends there. Should it make a difference if the product being sold is a TV or loaf of bread?

How about the risk involved in providing the product? A person who owns a store does not get paid as an employee. They get paid only if they sell enough of their product to cover all of their costs for the building, inventory, employees, taxes, etc. If they do not sell enough they lose money. Should this risk be factored in when determining if something is fair?

So far we have been focusing on fairness in terms of individuals. All of these issues become even more problematic when it comes to groups, to the point that fairness becomes whatever one wants it to be, or more importantly, does **not** want it to be. Any difference can be labeled unfair, and it is virtually impossible to counter such claims in any objective fashion, particularly, as we shall see shortly, when we move into the realm of politics.

Whereas over the centuries Justice has been improved by objective measures and standards such as written laws, clear rules of evidence, and unbiased judges in courts, Social Justice is a return to subjectivity, vague and impossible to define standards, and bias, in this case for the poor. Again, one might want to defend this out of concern for the poor, but it is not, and should not be confused with, Justice.

Where things get even more problematic, is when we move out of the world of theory, and start to put Social Justice into practice, particularly in the realm of politics. Politics is not a finely crafted instrument for precise tasks, particularly at the national level. It is at best a hammer, if not just a club. Thus as Social Justice moves from the books and articles of the theorists to the community activists and politicians it undergoes considerable simplification. This is not a criticism of activists and politicians; it is just the nature of politics in the modern world. The political realm has all the problems of Social Justice Theory, but these are often magnified as the theory is simplified, and the nuances and qualifications drop out.

In the political world, economic Social Justice distills down to "claims for the redistribution of resources" (Fraser, 1998). Notice that the policy of redistribution replaced the goals of equality and fairness. This is also a problem of Social Justice as frequently it comes with an automatic set of built-in solutions. As we will see in Part III, there are significant questions about the efficacy of these solutions. But in the political realm these solutions are, for the most part, unquestioned by the supporters of Social Justice.

In fact for many supporters any questioning of these supposed solutions is automatically equated, not only with opposition to Social Justice, but with a lack of concern for the poor, which is yet another key problem with Social Justice. At least within the political realm, it conflates Social Justice with concern for the poor and those in need. As a result, supporters of Social Justice frequently fall victim to the irrational fallacy of ad hominem attack as they demonize those who question their political policies as greedy, selfish, and uncaring.

This is one of the most pernicious of the logical fallacies for it is caustic to the open discussion needed to find the truth. Labels such as greedy and selfish are not only irrational, they are hardly conducive to a free exchange of ideas. Frequently, people who are called names do not react very well, particularly when they know they are false.

But such irrationalities also damage open discussion in that they put those who make such claims into a circle of self-justifying falsehoods, out of which it can be very difficult to escape. In this case, supporters of Social Justice call their opponents greedy, selfish and uncaring. Any protestations to the contrary are rejected. After all, if they cared, they would support the policies of Social Justice. So their protestations must be false, and their claims that they do care must be lies. When the opponent present evidence, such as will be present in Parts III and IV, the evidence is rejected or ignored. After all, why should one believe anything that a greedy, selfish, uncaring, and now untruthful person has to say? If they present studies and statistics, these are likewise rejected, normally with additional ad hominem attacks on those who did the studies.

As a critic of Social Justice, I personally have been on the receiving end of such "reasoning" many times, and my attempts to counter it have frequently been to no avail. Once, however, after several discussions and many hours on this subject with an acquaintance of mine, he finally got it, saying with a sense of astonishment, "You do care about the poor." Yes, I do, and so do many opponents of Social Justice.

One final problem with Social Justice, particularly in the realm of politics is the way that it stresses equality as a goal of government action. As a UN report put it, "Social justice is not possible without strong and coherent redistributive policies conceived and implemented by public agencies" including "a fair, efficient and progressive taxation system" (Department of Economic and Social Affairs, 2006, p. 6).

This brings with it all the problems of equality mentioned earlier, plus the additional problem of a conflict with liberty.[2] Here let me just summarize by pointing out that liberty and equality are, when it comes to government, mutually exclusive. The more a government stresses liberty, the less equality there will be. The more that government stress equality, the less liberty there will be. This is because the only way for government to ensure that people are equal is to restrict those things that lead to inequality.

Government puts limits on people in several ways. The first and most obvious is that the government can simply make certain activities illegal. However, they can also limit freedom by regulating how one must act, how one must use their land, how one must run their business. Another limit on liberty comes simply from taxation itself. Every dollar taken by the government is a dollar you are no longer free to spend. Your choices are limited simply because after taxes, you no longer have the money. Virtually everything government does limits freedom in one way, or another. Thus, the larger the government, the fewer freedoms people have.

This is the reason that supporters of Social Justice tend to be found on the left side of the political spectrum, and critics of Social Justice tend to be found on the right. It is not a concern for the poor or lack thereof. As a general rule, those on the left tend to seek solutions in government and value equality more than liberty. Those on the right, tend to seek solutions in the market and value liberty more than equality. Thus, what supporters of Social Justice mistakenly label a lack of concern for the poor, is actually just a different view of liberty vs. equality and a different approach to dealing with issues.

Social Justice is not the simple and positive virtue many assume it to be. While its goals are often noble, it has a darker side. It differs from the objectivity of Justice and instead seeks subjective measures of equality and fairness. As it moves into the political realm it conflates its goals of helping the poor with the ends of

2 For a more complete discussion of issues around liberty and equality see *Preserving Democracy*.

particular political policies, frequently demonizing opponents in the process. Ultimately its effort to achieve equality and fairness by means of expanding the role of government threatens liberty.

PART II: THE THEOLOGY OF SOCIAL JUSTICE

Not everyone advocating Social Justice does so for theological reasons, nor are those who do restricted to Christianity. But there are many who find justifications and even obligations for Social Justice in the Bible and that will be our focus here. At first glance, the case seems pretty clear and strong. As Commissioner Andrew Kalai of the Salvation Army writes, "We look at the Old Testament prophets and time and time again they raised their voice against oppression, injustice, dishonesty and corruption against the rulers of the ancient world, including Israel" (Kalai, 2014). In Amos 5:11 God pronounces judgment because "you trample the poor continuously." Zechariah 7:10 warns, "You are not to wrong the widow, orphans, the foreigner, or the poor, and you are not to plan evil against each other."

The New Testament likewise is very consistent. In Matthew 25:42-45 Jesus says,

> I was hungry, and you gave me nothing to eat. I was thirsty, and you gave me nothing to drink. [43]I was a stranger, and you didn't welcome me. I was naked, and you didn't clothe me. I was sick and in prison, and you didn't visit me.'
>
> [44]"Then they will reply, 'Lord, when did we see you hungry or thirsty or as a stranger or naked or sick or in prison and didn't help you?'
>
> [45]Then he will say to them, 'I tell all of you with certainty, since you didn't do it for one of the least important of these, you didn't do it for me.'

Another key verse is Galatians 3:28, "Because all of you are one in the Messiah Jesus, a person is no longer a Jew or a Greek, a slave or a free person, a male or a female." When it comes to concern for those who are disadvantaged, and to the equality of all, the message of both the Old Testament and New Testament is clear. But is this a solid foundation for Social Justice?

As we saw in Part I, Social Justice is more than this, particularly as it moves from theory into practice. So the real question is not whether the Bible does or does not teach that we should have a concern for the poor and disadvantaged as this is something shared by supporters and opponents of Social Justice alike. Instead, the question is whether or not it teaches economic equality and the corresponding focus on things such as fairness, and the particular political agenda supported by the advocates of Social Justice to achieve their goals.

While there is a debate as to just how early the word "fair" began to take on its modern meaning (Liberman, 2009), it is pretty clear that an equivalent Hebrew or Greek word does not appear in the Old or New Testament. When translations do use the word "fair" it translates the meaning of beautiful, such as the KJV's translation of the Song of Solomon 7:6 "How fair and how pleasant art thou…" or the weather as in the NIV's translation of Matthew 16:2, "It will be fair weather."

While the lack of the word casts doubt on the importance of the concept, it does not rule it out completely. In fact, there are places where fairness does seem to play a role. An example of this would be the parable of the workers in the vineyard found in Matthew 20:1-16. In this parable a landowner hires workers for his field in the morning, and then added more at various points during the day including just before that day's work ended. When the time came to pay the workers, all were paid the same amount, one denarius, regardless of how long they had worked. Those hired at the start of the day, "began to complain to the landowner, 'These last fellows worked only one hour, but you paid them the same as

us, and we've been working all day, enduring the scorching heat!'"
(Matthew 20:11-12).

Issues of fairness are in play here. But while this may offend
our sense of fairness, the Greek text says there was "no wrong" done,
something many modern translations do translate as not unfair
(Matthew 20:13). While the underlying message deals with heaven
rather than economics, it is one of the clearest passages to at least
touch on fairness. Given this, it is hard to claim that fairness plays
the central role that advocates of Social Justice have given it. The
Bible is concerned with the more objective right and wrong rather
than a subjective fair and unfair.[3] At best one might get a sort of
economic equality from this passage as they were all paid the same
amount, though it is clearly not equal pay for equal work. It does
reveal some of the problems with equality, for equal in one sense
often is inequality in another.

However, another parable has a different view of economic
equality. In the parable about the talents, a man leaves on a trip,
but before going he gives his servants various amounts of money.
"To one man he gave five talents, to another two, and to another
one, based on their ability" (Matthew 25:17). When he returned,
the servants showed what they had done with the money. The first
two had doubled the money and were rewarded. The servant who
had only received one talent, earned nothing and could only return
the talent back. Rather than equalize their money, the man took the
single talent away and gave it to the man who had the most money.

Again the parable is about the Kingdom of Heaven, not economics, so the messages are not really in conflict, but the point is
that they hardly paint a picture of equality. Perhaps, a better case
can be made from the description in Acts where,

> All the believers were united and shared everything with
> one another. [45]They made it their practice to sell their posses-
> sions and goods and to distribute the proceeds to anyone who

---

3 While the objectivity of morality is debated, the discussion is beyond the
scope of this book.

was in need. ⁴⁶United in purpose, they went to the Temple every day, ate at each other's homes, and shared their food with glad and humble hearts.

(Acts 2:44-46)

One of the issues here is that this seems to be more descriptive of what the early believers did, rather than something we are commanded to do. It certainly did not last very long, and later passages hint that it may have resulted in some problems. In Acts 11, we see Christians in Antioch taking up a collection for Judea. Later the Corinthians are also taking up gifts for Jerusalem. (1 Corinthians 16:3, 2 Corinthians 8:14) At the church in Thessalonica there were evidently those who were counting on the charity of others, causing Paul to write, "While we were with you, we gave this order: If anyone doesn't want to work, he shouldn't eat" (2 Thessalonians 3:10).

While the claims for fairness and economic equality are suspect, as the advocates of Social Justice move beyond concern and towards particular political policies, deeper issues emerge that are very problematic. As we saw in the first part, there is a difference between Justice and Social Justice and this is particularly true of Justice in the Bible.

An important aspect of biblical Justice is, "God does not show partiality" (Romans 2:11). In Deuteronomy the Israelites are told,

> Appoint judges and civil servants according to your tribes in all your cities that the LORD your God is about to give you, so they may judge the people impartially. ¹⁹You must not twist justice, show favoritism, or take bribes, because a bribe blinds the eyes of the wise and subverts the speech of the righteous. ²⁰You are to pursue justice—and only justice—so you may live and possess the land that the LORD your God is about to give you." (Deuteronomy 16:18-20)

Note that an aspect of Biblical Justice is impartiality. There are no exceptions. Yet, part of Social Justice is dividing people into various groups, primarily rich and poor and then advocating for one group over the other. As we saw in the first part, many advocates of Social Justice explicitly reject the concept of impartiality and give preference to the poor, but the Bible says, "You are not to be unjust in deciding a case. You are not to show partiality to the poor or honor the great. Instead, decide the case of your neighbor with righteousness" (Leviticus 19:15).

There are other problems as well. One is found in the tenth commandment, "You are not to covet your neighbor's house. You are not to covet your neighbor's wife, his male or female servant, his ox, his donkey, or anything that belongs to your neighbor" (Exodus 20:17). A major component of Social Justice is not only coveting, but taking from one group to give to another.

This is often justified by pointing to passages that speak of giving to the poor. Deuteronomy 15:11 says, "Since poor people won't cease to exist in the land, therefore, I'm commanding you: Be sure to be generous to your poor and needy relatives in your land." Jesus said, "Give to the person who asks you for something, and do not turn away from the person who wants to borrow something from you" (Matthew 5:42).

While this is indeed what we should do, there is a huge difference between giving, and having your money taken. In fact, I would submit, that it is impossible to fulfill these commandments through taxation. Despite what the money may be used for, having your money taken, particularly with automatic withholding, is just not the same thing as making the choice to give to the poor. Taxation is independent of any religious duty we might have, and thus cannot be justified on the basis of religious duty. There is certainly no religious duty to forcibly take money from others and give it to the poor.

Again, the advocates of Social Justice often label resistance to government programs for the poor as selfish, greedy and indicative of a lack of concern, yet this is countered by the well documented phenomena that those in groups that tend to support Social Justice give less to charity than those in groups that tend to oppose it. Most of this difference comes from the strong secular support for Social

Justice. While religious conservatives are slightly more likely to give, and give a little more than their liberal counterparts, both groups give far more than those who are secular.

The really big difference is that political liberals as a group tend to be more secular than their conservative counterparts. More secular means less giving (Brooks, *Who Really Cares*, 2007). Even if you focus just on those who are religious, the difference in giving is just not that significant, and if anything, actually gives the edge to those who oppose Social Justice.

This really should not be all that surprising. As Ralph Nader put it, "A society that has more justice is a society that needs less charity." While it is not true of many religious supporters of Social Justice, for many of the non-religious advocates, supporting Social Justice is a way to shield them from any obligation to deal with the problem of poverty themselves.

I believe the core injunction on this issue is to be found in 1 John 3:17-18,

> Whoever has earthly possessions and notices a brother in need and yet withholds his compassion from him, how can the love of God be present in him? [18]Little children, we must stop expressing love merely by our words and manner of speech; we must love also in action and in truth.

Given that the passage starts with "earthly possessions," it is somewhat surprising that the initial injunction concerns compassion rather than possessions. This is our primary responsibility: to have compassion for those in need. It is through this compassion that everything else must flow.

But our obligation does not stop there. Nor can it be fulfilled with words. Our compassion must work itself out "in action and in truth." The latter is again somewhat surprising. Rather than a statement that we must give of our possessions that one might expect, instead John speaks of actions and truth.

That we must act on our compassion is reasonable, and this will often involve sharing not only our possessions, but our time as well. But how does truth play into all this? I would argue that "truth" is the hardest part of the command. It is often very easy to think we can just give some money as if checking off a box, and thus fulfilling our obligation. But that is not a true working out of compassion. This is not to say that it is wrong, and in various circumstances it may be the best and most compassionate thing to do. But true compassion does not stop there.

True compassion is not centered on me, and whether or not I have fulfilled some obligation to the poor. True compassion is not done as something to make myself feel good; rather it is an investment into the lives of those in need. A true concern seeks to actually better the lives of those in need.

True compassion is concerned with results. Are lives actually improved? For short term needs such as those following a natural disaster like a flood, tornado or earthquake, short term results may be all that is needed. But for more long term problems just giving of our possessions may be ineffective, and, in fact, might even be counter-productive.

This is why religious injunctions are so out of place as a defense for government programs. Government, by its very nature and construction, measures success in terms of dollars spent and programs established, but rarely in terms of whether or not they are actually improving the lives of people. As we will see in the next section, the policies and programs supported by the advocates of Social Justice, while done with good intentions, often cause more harm than good.

PART III: THE FAILURES OF SOCIAL JUSTICE POLICIES

As we have seen, a key problem with many advocates of Social Justice is that they conflate concern for the poor with their particular policy proposals. But there is a large gap between concern for a problem and the results of a particular solution despite how reasonable that solution may seem.

During the early part of the 19th century, England was struggling with the transitions resulting from the Industrial Revolution and its corresponding surge of population into cities. One of the most notable side effects was the smell. Before the massive population explosion, London had dealt with the problem of human waste with "Night-Soil" men who would load it up on carts and take it to farms outside the city where it was used as fertilizer.

As the city grew, so did the distance to the farms, and so did the cost of transporting it. As a result, many people chose to simply let the waste fill up their basements, or pile up in an open part of their lot. Thus, it is not surprising that a feature of London frequently commented on during the period was the smell and it was by all accounts pretty bad. At the time, it was believed that the smell was not just obnoxious, but also posed a serious health risk. This is because the dominant theory of that time for diseases such as cholera was the Miasma theory, that disease was spread by bad air.

Progressives of the era, rightly concerned with the dismal conditions of the poor, sought to improve them by advocating the building of sewer systems to channel the waste, and thus the smell, away from the neighborhoods where people lived. In the middle part of the century many sewers were built. A noble cause with good intentions.

However, the sewers, while generally a good idea, were based on a faulty understanding of disease, and so their design was flawed. As bad as they were, the smells were not the cause for the epidemics of cholera that periodically swept through London. So they did nothing to stop them. What the new sewers did do is channel the sewage away from the neighborhoods and into the River Thames, which was also a major source of drinking water.

Thus rather than protect people from cholera, the new sewers actually made the problem worse. This is because cholera is a disease that produces extreme diarrhea to the point that those infected die of dehydration at times within hours of showing symptoms. It is transmitted by drinking water contaminated with the waste of cholera victims. So despite their good intentions, those seeking to save the poor from cholera ended up enabling cholera to spread much more effectively. The result was that tens of thousands of people died (Johnson, 2006).

The point here is not to be critical of those who pushed for the sewers but as a cautionary tale that we should not ignore results. And more importantly not assume that just because the intentions are good the resulting policies will produce the desired results, as they may, in fact, end up causing more harm than good.

Such is the case with many of the solutions proposed by the advocates of Social Justice. As with the Miasma theory for the spreading of disease, many of the theories behind the policies of Social Justice are seriously flawed. As a result, many of the proposed solutions actually do little to solve the problems they are intended to address, but rather simply make things worse.

Space does not permit a full analysis of the policies of Social Justice, but we will summarize the situation by focusing on three main problems, one with economics in general, one with the concept of profit and one with government, and then will look at a few examples.

At the core of the economic problems is a flawed understanding of wealth, in particular wealth creation and destruction. Ultimately all economic actions do one of two things. To one degree or another they either consume wealth, or they create wealth. The creation of wealth is conceptually pretty straight forward. Say, the raw materials and labor to make a loaf of bread are $0.45. If the loaf can be sold for $0.50, then baking a loaf of bread and selling it creates $0.05 of wealth.

While conceptually straightforward, there are two other factors involved, investment and risk. To see this consider the example just cited. If one wanted to become rich, in theory all they would have to do is bake enough loaves of bread. Want a million dollars? Then based on the example above just bake 20 million loaves of bread.

To do this, however, you would need to spend, that is invest, $9 million to get the raw materials and pay for the labor. No investment, no loafs of bread, no wealth creation. What if you did this and then could not sell all 20 million? What if you could only sell 10 million? In that case, rather than earning $1 million, you would in fact lose $4 million.[4] So not only do you have to invest $9 million, you have to risk $9 million with the hope that when all is said and done you will be able to sell enough loaves of bread to get your money back and then make some profit.

This is why a period of growth can be such a difficult and even dangerous time for a business. As orders increase, so will the need for raw materials and labor. Raw materials and labor normally cost much more than the expected profit. Thus, in our example, it took $0.45 to make $0.05. If the business grows too fast all the profit from the previous orders can be consumed by the raw materials and labor needed for the new orders. It is even possible the owner might have to borrow money in order to purchase raw materials and labor needed for the new orders. So unless managed carefully, growth can cause a lot of problems.

The key point here is that the growth of wealth is not an easy or simple thing to accomplish. Thus, it is not too surprising that most businesses fail within a few years. But when things are going well, and enough businesses are succeeding, then the economy grows.

Yet many of the solutions advocated by supporters of Social Justice are implicitly, and at times even explicitly, grounded in the idea that wealth is fixed. It cannot be created or destroyed, it can only be distributed. Often this is put in terms of a pie where everyone gets a portion. This is why inequality is seen as such a problem. For if one group gets too little of the pie, it must be because some other group is getting too much.

It is also why redistribution in one fashion or another is the standard solution in Social Justice. It is often dressed up with a lot of nice sounding language such as living wage, etc., but ultimately

---

4 The sale of 10 million loaves at $0.50 would result in $5 million. Since the 20 million loaf cost $9 million there would be a loss of $4 million.

it boils down to taking money from those who unfairly have too big a slice of the pie, and giving it to those who are being cheated from their fair share.

It is also why profit is seen as in some fashion tainted or even illegitimate. While workers are worthy of the money they earn, not so the owner. For many advocates of Social Justice, profit itself is equated with greed such that to seek profits is to be greedy. In areas such as health care, some consider profit downright immoral. This is why government is automatically to be preferred over business. Government, they believe, is not driven by the profit motive, as businesses are.

This is all based on a major misunderstanding of how the profit motive actually works. The profit motive does not produce greed, but concern for others. I realize that this may be a shocking statement to many supporters of Social Justice, but consider the following. Think of a restaurant or shop you like. Why do you like to go there? While there could be a variety of individual reasons, ultimately it is going to boil down to the fact that they are giving you something you want. In exchange, you give them something back, i.e. money.

It is this exchange, this mutual giving, that is at the core of the profit motive. In a true market based economy, a business has to provide a service or product that people want at a price that they are willing to pay to make a profit. Thus, the profit motive forces the business to be attentive to the needs of their customers. Ultimately what profit does is drive businesses to do things better for less money; to innovate and find new and better ways to deliver goods and services to their customers. If a business is only concerned with money, it will not stay in business very long unless it has some sort of protection from competition. But such protections normally come from government and are distortions of a market based economy.

This brings us to the final major theoretical problem: their view of government. As we have seen, for many advocates government is an integral part of Social Justice. It is just assumed to be working for the people because, unlike greedy businesses, government is not concerned about profit.

While this may sound nice in theory, it completely ignores the nature of bureaucracy and thus how government actually works. This view compares the loftiest goals of government, with the worst examples of business. To say that government is not interested in profit is, of course, true, because government does not have to worry about profit. But this also means that they do not need to be concerned about their "customers." If businesses do not provide good service, they will lose customers. If government doesn't, well you really have no choice when it comes to dealing with government.

Whereas businesses have a built-in incentive to lower costs, the incentive in government is exactly the opposite. Government is driven by power, and how much power one has is often a factor of how large one's budget is. This is just one of the reasons that the richest counties in the country are no longer near the centers of business, but now are near the centers of government. It is also why almost anything done by government costs more and gives you less than when done by the private sector.

Worse still, the larger government becomes, the more power it has, and the more it controls how things are done, the more corrupt it will become. If government doesn't do much, there is little to be gained by seeking to influence it. As government does more, the more there is to be gained. The bigger the bureaucracy becomes, the more people involved, the easier it will be to find someone willing to be influenced, and the easier it will be for the influence to go unnoticed.

The progressive reformer, Theodore Roosevelt, in his autobiography, recounts an incident where "a great railway corporation" wanted him to lead a bill through the NY legislature because he was well known to be honest and "nothing improper" would be done to get the bill passed. While "the municipal authorities and the property-owners whose property was to be taken favored it" (Roosevelt, 1920, p. 40) the bill was blocked by corrupt politicians.

Eventually control of the bill had to be given to another politician who would not be as vigilant about doing things the right way. As Roosevelt summed up the incident, people were just not as concerned "so long as only the corporations were blackmailed" (Roosevelt, 1920, p. 41).

Influence is not always business going after government, government frequently wants to be sought. In its early years, Microsoft was pretty much apolitical. It went about its business without any real lobbying effort. Then the government went after it for anti-trust violations. Now it has learned its lesson and has hired lobbyists.

Like the Miasma theory at the beginning of this section, the flawed theories behind much of Social Justice mean that, despite its advocates' good intentions, their policies often end up causing more harm than good. Take, for example, the frequent calls to raise the minimum wage, or as it is now being called, a living wage.

Every few years this issue bubbles up to the surface. On its face the argument sounds compassionate. Supporters of an increase point to how little the current minimum wage is, how long it has been since it was last raised, how many workers would be affected, how many it would lift out of poverty, and other such arguments. Frequently these are tied to the arguments of Social Justice with statements such as "with corporate profits soaring, it would be fair if companies would share some of the wealth with their hard-working employees at the bottom rung – the ones who actually do the lion's share of the work – but don't count on it" (Magliano, 2014).

If raising the minimum wage is so positive why would anyone be against it? Often supporters see it simply as, "corporate greed and government indifference" (Magliano, 2014), an example of the lack of openness to differing views discussed earlier. Actually, if one is concerned with the poor, there are several good reasons to oppose an increase in the minimum wage. In addition, as we will see in the next section, there is a much better way to deal with these problems.

The policy of increasing the minimum wage is grounded in the fundamental misunderstanding of economics discussed above.

Most economic action either creates wealth or consumes it to one degree or another. When someone creates bread and sells it, wealth is created. Creating bread and failing to sell it such that there is a loss, destroys wealth. Paying workers, while an important part of the process does not in and of itself create wealth. The wealth is created when the product is sold for a price greater than the cost of production.

Thus, raising the minimum wage does not create wealth, it transfers it. Again you can see the idea of a fixed economic pie lurking in the background. The business owners are taking too much of the pie, so government must step in and force a transfer of wealth from the owner to the employees.

Since no wealth is created, raising the minimum wage will have some combination of the following. 1) The owner must do with less. 2) The owner must cut costs. 3) The owner must raise prices. Given that most businesses fail anyway, option one is at best questionable. Option two assumes there are existing costs that could be cut, but were not, i.e. that the business was wasting money. Again this is very questionable.

If a business does cut, it will most likely cut employees, and thus some people will not see their wages increased but rather see them cut to zero. Even if the owner decides to do with less, their primary goal will be to regain what was lost, and so will most likely delay future hiring. Raising the minimum wage will cost jobs.

Since the increase in the minimum wage covers all employers, option three is a possibility, as the competition might increase their prices as well, but this all depends on people's willingness to pay the higher prices. For example, many restaurant owners know that if they raise prices, people frequently respond by 'moving down the menu,' i.e., they simply purchase cheaper items.

Option three also defeats the purpose of increasing the minimum wage in the first place, as an increase in prices can wipe out any benefit from an increased minimum wage. Yet, while such an increase may end up being a wash for employees as their increased pay is offset by increased prices, those on fixed incomes end up suffering. There is also the issue of those who have worked hard to earn more than minimum wage suddenly finding themselves back at minimum wage.

There is another group that suffers as well. When an employer hires an employee, it is because they have a job that needs to be done. All jobs have an economic value to the employer, in that the work done by the employee will help towards the goal of providing a good and/or service to the customer. If an employer has a potential job, but one that is not worth the minimum wage, then that job will not be created and the person will not be hired. This is a serious problem, for a minimum wage is also a starting wage. It allows a person to enter the work force and learn the skills needed to earn a higher wage. But if they cannot get started, this can never happen.

Whereas advocates of Social Justice focus on the wages of employees going up with an increase in the minimum wage, the actual results will be more complex. While some employers will do with less, some employees will lose their jobs while increased prices wipe out the benefit of the increase. Those on fixed incomes and those wanting to be hired will suffer.

Given the size and complexity of the economy, the exact effects of any particular increase can be difficult to measure, especially given the normal swings in the economy. Also, it is very likely that different sectors of the economy and country will see different combinations of these results. This is particularly true given the size of the increase when compared to the size of the economy, as most workers already make more than minimum wage. But that these problems are small and difficult to measure does not mean that they do not exist and can be ignored.

The problems with raising the minimum wage can be seen with a simple thought experiment. At the time I am writing, the Federal minimum wage is $7.25 per hour, and there are various proposals to raise it to $9.00 or higher. If raising it is such a good thing, then why not make it $100 per hour? It is pretty clear that this would result in the problems mentioned above. But a smaller "more reasonable" increase does not mean that the problems disappear, it just means that they are easier to ignore, unless of course you are one of those that loses their job, or cannot get a job, or is on a fixed income and has to struggle with higher prices, or one of the business owners who lose their business because the increased labor costs priced them out of the market.

The last item we will look at is, as we saw in the UN statement in the first section, one of the main vehicles of wealth redistribution: the progressive income tax. The progressive income tax again sounds good on the surface; those with the most money should pay the most in taxes. But it has serious problems not only economically, but morally and politically was well.

One problem for a progressive income tax is found in its very purpose, for it confuses the concepts of income and wealth. To see this consider the following example: Mary has $10 million dollars and does not work, as she earns an income of $100,000 from investments. Joe has no savings, but works hard and earned $150,000. Who has the most money? Easy, Mary. But for the purposes of the income tax, Joe has more.

Then there is the issue of when income is earned. Say Joe is an author who writes a book every three years. The book sells well in the year it is released, but very little after that. So every three years Joe earns his $150,000 but he has to live on that for three years as he writes his next book. That is a yearly income of $50,000, half of what Mary earns, but for income tax purposes he is taxed at a higher rate, much more than if he actually earned $50,000 each year.

We will come to the other economic problems shortly, but first let me touch on the moral and political problems. To understand the moral problem consider the following hypothetical people: Sam and Bob. Sam has money, Bob does not, so he goes to Sam and takes some of his money by force. The problem here is easy to see: Bob has stolen Sam's money. What if instead of going alone, Bob gets a number of his friends together and they go take some of Sam's money by force, and then divide it up among themselves? This really does not change things, and it is still theft. So how is it that using the cloak of government, the majority can do the same thing, i.e., take money by force from those who have it so as to redistribute it?

Normally the answer has something to do with sharing the burden, but by definition a progressive income tax is not a shared burden. This is not everyone agreeing to tax themselves a certain percentage of their income in order to fund the needed work of government. This is a majority agreeing to take money from a minority. As I cite in my book *Preserving Democracy*, the top 10% of wage earners earn 46% of the income but pay 67% of the income taxes. The bottom 50% paid less than 4% of the income taxes, and, in fact, the lowest 40% as a group actually get more back in the form of tax credits than they paid in.

This creates a political imbalance that as very dangerous for a democratic system of government. There is very little cost to increased spending for the majority, after all they are only paying a very small part of the bill if anything. Inevitably this will result in fiscal collapse, such as we have already seen in various countries.

This brings us back to the economic problems. The rich in modern economies do not lock up their wealth in vaults. Instead, they have it invested where it will hopefully grow, creating new wealth. But redistribution does not create wealth. Quite the opposite, every dollar redistributed is a dollar taken from wealth creation.

This is one of the problems with focusing on economic equality in the first place. As discussed earlier, the creation of wealth is an inherently risky endeavor. Most who try fail, but the few who succeed earn great rewards. This alone is going to create inequality in wealth. It does not really matter whether this income is earned, is simply a matter of being in the right place at the right time, or just dumb luck (I think all are involved). What matters is that while a growing and vibrant economy produces inequality, it allows everyone to do better.

Redistribution of income may sound kind and compassionate; take money from those who have it and give it to those that need it, but it distorts the economy. It uses money that otherwise would have been invested to grow the economy. It not only reduces the reward of succeeding, but it also makes it harder to succeed in the first place. This is because the first place an emerging business invests is in its own growth. But if that money is redistributed, the growth that money would have funded is lost.

Thus, the move towards equality is not achieved by lifting the poor up, but rather by holding others back. It is an equality of the bottom, not an equality of the top. The more equality is sought, the less the economy can grow and over time even the poor will end up worse off than they would have been. Ultimately it makes matters worse, so that states which enact Social Justice policies actually end up with greater inequality than states which don't (Moore & Vedder, 2014). If pushed too much, the economy will contract and if that happens it will be the poor who suffer the most.

The final problem with seeking such solutions in government is that the government is a major cause of the problem. This is simply because the larger government is, the more tax dollars it will need and the more regulation it will produce. Every dollar taken in taxes is one less dollar that can be invested in growth. Every regulation is a limit on innovation that can result in new and better ways of doing things.

Often advocates of Social Justice put things in terms of Wall Street vs. Main Street; Big business vs. the little guy. They claim that we need government to level the playing field. What they fail to realize is that a lot of the time, big business likes government regulation. This is because the regulations often try to lock in "best practices," and the best practices normally are the way that larger businesses are already operating. This insulates them from smaller businesses coming up with new and innovative ways of doing things, ways that might be better and thus make inroads into the market share of the more established businesses.

Government regulations also set up many barriers to entry, things a business must do before they can enter a market, which again helps to limit the competition. Finally big business can more easily afford the cost of compliance as they have the lawyers and lobbyists needed to navigate the bewildering mazes of government bureaucracy. So a large government frequently is more an ally of the biggest businesses against the smaller ones than the other way around.

This cost of complying with government regulations has grown steadily over the last century and by 2008 reach a staggering $1.75 trillion dollars. That was 12 percent of the Gross National Product, and again this is just the cost of complying with regulations. Arthur C. Brooks, President of the American Enterprise Institute, points out that for a small business with just 19 workers, complying with all this regulation costs $10,585 per worker. This means the business must make $201,115 just to pay for this regulation (Brooks, *The Road To Freedom*, 2012).

There is a very simple rule in economics that should be obvious to all. Raising the cost of something will reduce that thing. This is the theory behind cigarette taxes. Increase the cost of smoking and fewer people will smoke, and those who do will tend to smoke less. Whatever your views on cigarette taxes, they have had this effect on smoking. The same thing applies to economic growth. Increase the cost of running a business, either through increase taxes, or increased regulation, and there will be slower growth, i.e. less wealth creation and fewer employees hired. Increase it too much and you will have a recession.

It should not be a surprise that as government has grown, increasing the burden on businesses through taxes and regulation, economic growth has been on a downward path. While going back to the early fifties growth well above 6 percent used to be common, the last time it occurred was in the early 1980s. The seemingly strong growth of the late 1990s internet bubble didn't even reach 5 percent. The strongest growth so far this century was only 3.9 percent (Commerce, 2014).

This is the problem with the Social Justice approach of relying on government. The more it does, the greater the burden on the economy and thus the less growth there will be. The less growth, the more the problems of unemployment and poverty will grow and thus the more government will need to do. Over time, this sets up a death spiral that will end in fiscal collapse if not reversed.

The problems of Social Justice are not to be found in its advocates' concern for those in need, which is noble and good, but rather in the ambiguity of fairness, the elusiveness of economic equality, a flawed understanding of economics, and in the reliance on a growing government that seeks solutions through redistribution. The bottom line of all of this is that the policies and approaches pushed by advocates of Social Justice ultimately end up promising more than they can deliver. While done in the name of compassion, there is no compassion in an empty promise. With the size of government already reducing economic growth, with taxes and national debt all at record highs, and with Medicare and Social Security facing bankruptcy, we are well on the way to fiscal collapse. There must be a better way.

PART IV: A BETTER APPROACH

The policy failures of Social Justice should not be taken to mean that nothing can be done. A better approach would start by abandoning the goal of economic equality and instead focus on economic mobility, the ability to move up. After all, which is more important, that those in need have their needs met and that the poor are given a way out of poverty or that some arbitrary level of equality is obtained?

What is needed is an approach that focuses more on causes (lack of economic growth and opportunity) than on symptoms (poverty). When we look at the poor, the first question is not how can we give them money, but rather why are they poor? If they cannot work for some reason, then this is clearly a place for welfare. If they could work, but cannot find a job, then the question becomes why are there no jobs? If they have a job but are not earning enough, then the question becomes, why can't they find a better paying job?

In short, these are problems of economic growth, not income inequality. The solution is not the creation of an elaborate and costly system of redistribution, but rather a healthy and growing economy that provides people with choices and options, an economy where one can move up the economic ladder.

When there is an oversupply of labor, i.e., more people looking for work than there are jobs, unemployment will be pushed up, and wages will be pushed down. A minimum wage can mask the decline in wages by putting in an artificial floor, but nothing is free and, as we have seen, the price will be paid.

As a side note, another counterproductive policy frequently supported by Social Justice advocates is a lax enforcement of the border that permits an influx of workers, many of whom are low skilled. Adding such workers to the labor pool can only depress wages further, increase unemployment even more, and create an underground economy where workers can more easily be exploited. Again, what is done in compassion, results in further suffering.

Rather than masking these problems with a minimum wage increase or extended unemployment insurance benefits, a better approach is to ask why the economy is not growing faster? The idea that a growing economy can solve these problems is not just an abstract economic theory, but a real solution that actually works.

To see this, just consider the situation in North Dakota. At the time I am writing, we are in the sixth year of a stagnating economy with growth around 1-2 percent. Millions are struggling to find work, and many have just given up. Many of those who do find a job complain about low wages or limited hours. While unemployment has dropped, it has dropped more from people leaving the workforce than from people finding jobs. In a recent job report, 288,000 people found jobs, but 800,000 left the job market (Sherk, 2014). Sadly this is not an exception but has been the case in all but 2 months since 2009.

Yet while people struggle to find work, the situation in North Dakota is the exact opposite. As a result of the discovery of the

Bakken oil reserves, the economy in North Dakota is booming and anyone who wants a job can find one. In fact, employers, not workers, are the ones struggling. As a result, nobody cares about the minimum wage debate in Washington D.C., or a proposal to raise it to $9.00. This is because employers are so desperate to find people that workers "can make $15 an hour serving tacos, $25 an hour waiting tables and $80,000 a year driving trucks" (Ellis, 2011).

More importantly, the economy does not have to be growing as much as North Dakota to eliminate the need for a minimum wage. A steady growth of four or five percent will, after a period of time, leave employers who pay wages at the low end of the pay scale struggling to find workers and having to pay higher than minimum wage. This is because a good economy opens up job opportunities at all wage levels and so good workers are in demand. They seek and can find better paying jobs.

Our focus should be on the economy and job creation. Get that right and a significant part of the poverty problem will take care of itself. This will not take care of the entire problem as not all causes of poverty are based in economics. Situations such as single parent households, or destructive behaviors like compulsive gambling and drug addiction also play roles in poverty, but they are outside the scope of this book. Still, even here there would be some benefit, as a strong economy with a labor shortage is far more likely to be flexible for workers with child care needs than a depressed economy where unemployment is high and employers can be picky about whom they hire.

So if we want a strong economy, how do we go about it? First, to counter some typical canards and straw men that are usually raised about this point, this is not a call to get rid of government. True, as we saw in the last section, government is currently a major problem. But it does not follow that we should get rid of government. Government does have a very important role to play.

The key issue is not so much government in and of itself, but rather what is it doing, and how big it is. When it comes to the economy, there are simply too many factors to take into consideration to allow for top-down management. Even if one looks at just a segment of the economy such as energy or perhaps food production, things very quickly get very, very complex. In reality, such segments are themselves artificial as there is a tremendous overlap. Food production consumes a lot of energy and also is a major factor in the production of ethanol.

The only way to "manage" the economy is from the bottom up. Such management does not exclude government, but it does transform its role, and limit its size. The role for government in such a system is two-fold. First government must establish a framework in which the economy can function. This consists of mundane things such as law and order, clear and consistent legal frameworks, the definition of what are and are not legal practices, and a system in which disputes can be worked out. Note the word "framework" here. While government would certainly act directly in a number of these areas, this would not rule out non-governmental options such as binding arbitration.

The other main area would be to encourage a business environment where there was real competition and customers had real choices, in short capitalism. Often this is distorted as just looking out for business. It is not. The focus is not on what is best for business, but rather, what is best for consumers. Businesses must compete and consumers must have real choices.

Perhaps the closest model here would be with food. While for those in need we have assistance programs, access to food is largely left to the market. As a result, we have what as little as 50 years ago would be seen as an unbelievable amount of choice. In terms of stores, we can choose between a range of large stores, discount stores and a wide variety of specialty stores. Then again we can choose to get hot dogs at the gas station, or take-out, or fast food, or we could choose to go to a sit-down restaurant. But even here our choices are still varied and numerous, from sports bars, to cafés to simple restaurants, to expensive steak houses, and all of this before you consider the range of regional and national foods and even specialty restaurants. This is how market forces, governed

31

by choice and competition, work themselves out, and it does work, when government allows it to.

Such economic systems have a lot of inequality, but in exchange, provide us a vast number of choices for questions as simple as "What do we want for dinner tonight?" It also provides millions of people with jobs and has created a tremendous amount of wealth, which enriches us all. Nor are such policies limited to Western economies. As Arthur C. Brooks has pointed out because of such policies, "The number of people in the world living on a dollar a day—a traditional poverty measure—has fallen by 80 percent since 1970, from 11.2 percent of the world's population to 2.3 percent" (Brooks, *The Road To Freedom*, 2012, p. 72). Where such polices are on the rise, poverty has fallen the fastest.

Space does not permit a full discussion of all the benefits, but there are two more I want to at least briefly mention. The first is liberty. An economy built around choice and competition will permit far more freedom. It is just a fact that the freedom to choose is greater when there are more things to choose from, and this requires a growing economy. Even if the policies of Social Justice could bring more equality, it would be with at a cost of liberty.

The final benefit is the clear and definite link between earned success and happiness. "If the government gives people rewards they did not earn—welfare checks, make-work jobs, or whatever—it will not improve their well-being. Even worse, it will make them helpless" (Brooks, *The Road To Freedom*, 2012, p. 30). The point here is that earned success leads to happiness, and earned success is most likely to happen in an economy that is both growing and dynamic enough that it allows people the freedom to make the choices that are best for them. Abandoning the policies of Social Justice will not only allow people to be better off, but they will in general be happier and, in the end, that is more important than material equality.

Further Reading

Preserving Democracy, Hushbeck, Elgin (2010), Gonzalez, FL Energion

Wealth and Poverty, Gilder, George (2012) Washington DC: Regnery

The Road To Freedom. Brooks, A. C. (2012) New York: Basic Books.

Works Cited

Brooks, A. C. (2007). *Who Really Cares.* Basic Books.

Brooks, A. C. (2012). *The Road To Freedom.* New York: Basic Books.

Commerce, U. D. (2014). *National Economic Accounts. Retrieved from Bureau of Economic Analysis:* http://www.bea.gov/national/index.htm#gdp

Department of Economic and Social Affairs. (2006). *Social Justice in an Open World.* 2006: United Nations.

Ellis, B. (2011, October 20). *Double your salary in the middle of nowhere, North Dakota.* Retrieved from CNN Moneyh: http://money.cnn.com/2011/09/28/pf/north_dakota_jobs/index.htm

Fraser, N. (1998, December). *Social Justice in the Age of Identity Politics: Redistribution, Recognition, Participation.* Retrieved from www.econstor.eu: http://www.econstor.eu/bitstream/10419/44061/1/269802959.pdf

Johnson, S. (2006). *The Ghost Map.* Riverhead Trade.

Kalai, A. (2014, May). *Biblical Reflections on Social Justice Advocacy.* Retrieved from The Salvation Army International Social Justice Commission : http://www1.salvationarmy.

org/IHQ/www_ihq_isjc.nsf/vw-dynamic-index/EEF8C-4C334233FE2802578AF00525772?openDocument

Kennedy, R. (2010, 12 15). *That Lady With the Scales Poses for Her Portraits*. Retrieved from New York Times Books: http://www.nytimes.com/2010/12/16/books/16justice.html?_r=0

Liberman , M. (2009, January 28). *No word for fair?* Retrieved from Language Log: http://languagelog.ldc.upenn.edu/nll/?p=1080

Magliano, T. (2014, January 30). *ECONOMIC JUSTICE: Raising the minimum wage, an economic and moral necessity*. Retrieved from Pax Christi USA: http://paxchristiusa.org/2014/01/30/economic-justice-raising-the-minimum-wage-an-economic-and-moral-necessity/

Moore, S., & Vedder, R. (2014, June 4). The Blue-State Path to Inequality. *Wall Street Journal*. Retrieved from http://online.wsj.com/articles/stephen-moore-and-richard-vedder-liberal-blue-states-have-greater-income-inequality-than-conservative-red-states-1401923793

Prager, D. (2012). *Still the Best Hope: Why the World Needs American Values to Triumph*. HarperCollins.

Robinson, M. (2014, 4 23). *What is Social Justice?* Retrieved from Appalachian State University Department of Government and Justice Studies: http://gjs.appstate.edu/social-justice-and-human-rights/what-social-justice

Roosevelt, T. (2011-03-24). Theodore Roosevelt; an Autobiography (p. 41). Kindle Edition.

Sherk, J. (2014, May 2). *Jobs Report: Unemployment Down, But 800,000 Leave Workforce*. Retrieved from The Foundry: http://blog.heritage.org/2014/05/02/jobs-report-unemployment-800000-leave-workforce/

Topical Line Drives

Straight to the Point in under 44 Pages

All Topical Line Drives volumes are priced at $4.99 print and 99¢ in all ebook formats.

Available

The Authorship of Hebrews: The Case for Paul	David Alan Black
What Protestants Need to Know about Roman Catholics	Robert LaRochelle
What Roman Catholics Need to Know about Protestants	Robert LaRochelle
Forgiveness: Finding Freedom from Your Past	Harvey Brown, Jr.
Process Theology: Embracing Adventure with God	Bruce Epperly
Holistic Spirituality: Life Transforming Wisdom from the Letter of James	Bruce Epperly
To Date or Not to Date: What the Bible Says about Pre-Marital Relationships	D. Kevin Brown
The Eucharist: Encounters with Jesus at the Table	Robert D. Cornwall
Rendering unto Caesar	Chris Surber
The Caregiver's Beatitudes	Robert Martin

Forthcoming

God the Creator: The Variety of Christian Views on Origins	Henry Neufeld
The Authority of Scripture in a Postmodern Age: Some Help from Karl Barth	Robert D. Cornwall

Planned

A Cup of Cold Water	Chris Surber
Christian Existentialism	David Moffett-Moore
Paths to Prayer	David Moffett-Moore
I'm Right and You're Wrong	Steve Kindle

(The titles of planned volumes may change before release.)

Generous Quantity Discounts Available
Dealer Inquiries Welcome
Energion Publications — P.O. Box 841
Gonzalez, FL 32560
Website: http://energionpubs.com
Phone: (850) 525-3916

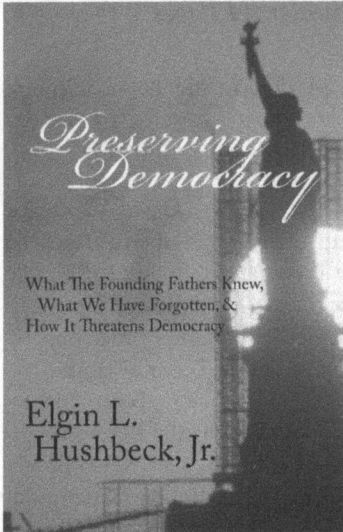

Every citizen who seeks to be not merely informed but also inspired ought to read it.

W. B. Allen
Emeritus Professor of
Political Philosophy
Michigan State University

ALSO BY ELGIN HUSHBECK, JR.

Elgin Hushbeck has produced one of the best books available today to put into the hands of the educated skeptic.

Craig J. Hazen
Director of MA Program
in Christian Apologetics
Biola University

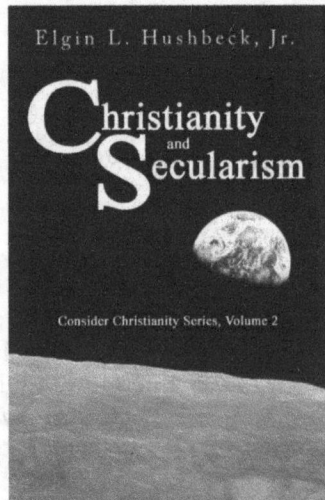

MORE FROM ENERGION PUBLICATIONS

Personal Study
The Jesus Paradigm	David Alan Black	$17.99
When People Speak for God	Henry Neufeld	$17.99

Christian Living
Faith in the Public Square	Robert D. Cornwall	$16.99
Grief: Finding the Candle of Light	Jody Neufeld	$8.99
Crossing the Street	Robert LaRochelle	$16.99

Bible Study
Learning and Living Scripture	Lentz/Neufeld	$12.99
From Inspiration to Understanding	Edward W. H. Vick	$24.99
Luke: A Participatory Study Guide	Geoffrey Lentz	$8.99
Philippians: A Participatory Study Guide	Bruce Epperly	$9.99
Ephesians: A Participatory Study Guide	Robert D. Cornwall	$9.99
Evidence for the Bible	Elgin Hushbeck, Jr.	

Theology
Creation in Scripture	Herold Weiss	$12.99
Creation in Contemporary Experience	David Moffett-Moore	$9.99
Ultimate Allegiance	Robert D. Cornwall	$9.99
History and Christian Faith	Edward W. H. Vick	$9.99
The Church Under the Cross	William Powell Tuck	$11.99
Philosophy for Believers	Edward W. H. Vick	$14.99
Christianity and Secularism	Elgin Hushbeck, Jr.	$16.99

Ministry
Clergy Table Talk	Kent Ira Groff	$9.99
So Much Older Then ...	Robert LaRochelle	$9.99

Politics
Preserving Democracy	Elgin L. Hushbeck, Jr.	$14.99
Faith in the Public Square	Robert D. Cornwall	$16.99

Generous Quantity Discounts Available
Dealer Inquiries Welcome
Energion Publications — P.O. Box 841
Gonzalez, FL 32560
Website: http://energionpubs.com
Phone: (850) 525-3916

www.ingramcontent.com/pod-product-compliance
Lightning Source LLC
Chambersburg PA
CBHW011750020426
42331CB00014B/3344